TRANSFORMATION

IS

AN INSIDE JOB

_____

This book belongs to

_____

Date

No part of this publication may be reproduced, distributed or transmitted in any form or by any means, including photocopying recording or other electronic or mechanical methods or by any information storage and retrieval system without the prior written permission of the publisher, except in the case of brief quotation embodied in critical reviews and specific other non-commercial uses permitted by copyright law.

Under no circumstances will any blame or legal responsibility be held against the publisher or author, for any damages, reparation, or monetary loss due to the information contained within this book. Either directly or indirectly.

Disclaimer Notice

Please note the information contained within this document is for educational and entertainment purposes only. All effort has been executed to present accurate, up to date, and reliable, complete information. No warranties of any kind are declared or implied. Readers acknowledge that the author is not engaging in the rendering of legal, financial, medical or professional advice. The content within this book has been derived from various sources. Please consult a licensed professional before attempting any techniques outlined in this book.

By reading this document, the reader agrees that under no circumstances is the author responsible for any loses, direct or indirect, which are incurred as a result of the use of information contained within this document, including, but not limited to, - errors, omissions, or inaccuracies.

ACKNOWLEDGEMENTS

This workbook is the result of my personal, professional and ministerial experience of working with women for well over three decades. I firmly believe that when women come together, we become better and truly demonstrate that "iron sharpens iron". As women, we often take care of everyone, except ourselves and are left with holes in our hearts and souls. This workbook is the product of my personal transformation of learning how to close those holes, reject stinking thinking, stinking opinions and stinking self-talk by renewing my mind, thoughts and speech with affirming self-talk, and establishing a sphere of women, that will keep you accountable, integrity driven, and determined to live by your core values (you know who you are, thank you).

Billy, my encourager and teammate of over 36 years, thank you for listening to me talk for hours about women's issues, never getting tired, and pushing me to share, write and ask tons of questions. You are The WHY to my living FORWARD.

To my children, BJ, Tarshuma and Darius thank you for sharing me with others. I am because of each of you. To my Nana pudding Rylan, my Cammy girl, and Chad (my peanut). To my adopted grown adults, Tanya, Kathy, Denise, Veniece, thank you for years of dreaming out loud with me.

To my amazing mother, Almerrier and my sister Denise, for your support and the many days of listening to my thoughts and giving me feedback. To my brother for always saying yes to my ideas and last minute requests. To the man that pushed me and made it sound so simple, because he was willing to do all the heavy lifting, my nephew TR Burns (Kingdom Guru), you are truly a gift to the kingdom.

To Love Fellowship Tabernacle – The Kingdom Church, Bishop Hezekiah Walker, thank you for allowing me to work out my gifting and callings.

To all of the "Transformation" ladies that walked through this journey and allowed me to walk side by side with them as they transformed - you ladies will always be my She-ro.

Table of Contents

INTRODUCTION 1

IT'S MY LIFE ~ WEEK ONE 16

IT'S MY LIFE ~ WEEK TWO 35

IT'S MY LIFE ~ WEEK THREE 54

IT'S MY LIFE ~ WEEK FOUR 73

IT'S MY LIFE ~ WEEK FIVE 92

IT'S MY LIFE ~ WEEK SIX 111

IT'S MY LIFE ~ WEEK SEVEN 130

IT'S MY LIFE ~ WEEK EIGHT 149

IT'S MY LIFE ~ WEEK NINE 168

BIBLIOGRAPHY 185

Introduction

In the pages ahead, you will take a deeper look into the most important person in your life, **YOU**.

Have you ever asked yourself "**WHO AM I**" and had no clue how to answer yourself? You may have taken on so many personas, that you have lost yourself along the way.

Knowing who you are is the most critical step in building your confidence muscle. In this workbook, you are encouraged to discover who you are on a deeper level so you can appreciate yourself at a higher level. When you can better understand yourself; what makes how and what you do unique based on what and how you think, you will gain a better understanding of your decision-making process.

I am a transformed lady, who lives each day with an expectation to grow, to do and to become the woman I want to be.

The following are building blocks needed for transformation:
- Clarity
- Focus
- Intentionality
- Application
- Self-awareness

How to Get the Most from Using Workbook

Change can be hard. It requires no extra effort to settle for the same old thing. Auto-pilot keeps us locked into past patterns. But transforming your life? That requires courage, commitment, and effort. It's tempting to stay camped in the zone of That's-Just-How-It-Is. But to get to the really good stuff in life, you have to be willing to become an explorer and adventurer. -- John Mark Green

This workbook was created as a proactive tool towards inner growth. These exercises should be completed at your own pace. Work through them thoughtfully and slowly – but **DO** work through them.

We cannot move forward without looking inward. When we look inward, it now requires action:

Weekly Scripture to Memorize

At the beginning of each week, you will be assigned a scripture to memorize. I recommend writing it on a 3x5 index card, carry it with you, and read the verse over and over out loud.

Weekly Prayers

You will be assigned a scripture-based prayer each week, which you are to pray slowly every day. Add to the prayer your own feelings and prayer request for the week. Say your pray out loud daily.

Share my Heart Prayer

Write a prayer from your heart to God.

Weekly Affirmation

Look into the mirror and recite the assigned affirmation at the beginning of each week.

Personal Affirmation

Each week write your own affirmation, repeat it and make it manifest each day.

What is my intention for this week?

List what you will do intentionally for the week.

The way I will manifest it this week?

Write out the steps you will take to accomplish your intention for this week.

My Weekly Schedule will look like?

Schedule all your appointments and everything you want to do.

I Will

This statement requires you to own it and make intentional changes in that area.

Detox

This area will require you to look deeper into what needs to be detoxed in or out of your life.

Write One of Your Core Values

List one of your core values.

How is it showing up?

Express how that core value is showing up in your life.

What is one priority?

List one priority that you want to accomplish this week.

What Action?

What action and/or actions will it take for you to accomplish your priority for this week?

Self-Care

There are many different options when it comes to self-care. It should always be a method that feels right for you. Self-care is essential in helping to reduce the chaos and unpredictability that undermines your ability to parent, work or even function on a daily basis.

The basic needs approach involves any physical aspect of treating your body well so you can function each day.

The comfort/pleasure approach can be anything that brings you joy or gives you a sense of ease. Through self-care, you will feel better.

I AM

The power of the I AM Statement - it is a command to your mind to produce what it states.

What's your I AM statement for each week?

Create your statement to live by each week. Speak it every morning, noon and night. Your I AM Statement will build weekly and begin to speak into your life. Each week that you build them, add on from the other weeks.

Question?

You have seven days of questions; one question per day to answer and/or follow through the activities that accompany each question. Please dig deep. You have the power to go deeper or stay surface. It's up to **YOU**!

Conclusion of Week

What is your experience this week?

Why? What was happening, to make you feel or think that way?

I am grateful for what this week?

What I learned about myself this week?

What vision about **YOU** have you seen in a different or the same light? What actions about **YOU** do **YOU** want to make better or stay the same? What perception of **YOU** do you need to change? What things about **YOU** did you find or lose? What things about **YOU** have excited **YOU**? What characteristics about **YOU** have you loved in a better way?

Why is it important for **YOU** not to just change but to **Transform**? According to the Merriam-Webster dictionary, *transformation* means "a complete or major change in someone or something's appearance, form, etc."

In the New Testament, the Greek word for *transformation* is *metamorphosis*. The definition of *metamorphosis* is: "a profound change in form from one stage to the next in the **life** history of an organism, as from the caterpillar to the pupa and from the pupa to the adult butterfly."

A caterpillar is born already possessing the life that will cause it to become a butterfly. Although an outward change does occur during metamorphosis, it's the result of an organic change from within. A caterpillar doesn't put on a butterfly costume or strive to act like a butterfly. As long as it eats, a caterpillar can trust in the metabolic process to assimilate those nutrients into its body and cause it to grow. Eventually, it undergoes metamorphosis and becomes a butterfly.

We can't transform ourselves by simply making up our minds to do so. But as *Romans 12:2* tells us, *Do not be conformed to this world, but be transformed by the renewal of your mind, that by testing you may discern what is the will of God, what is good and acceptable and perfect.* We can be transformed; that is, we can cooperate with the Lord to allow this process of transformation to take place. in us. Transformation is not a one-time deal and you're done - it requires daily self-awareness.

Psalm 139:23-24 Search me, O God, and know my heart! Try me and know my thoughts! And see if there be any grievous way in me, and lead me in the way everlasting! Show me, ME. Stop and take a closer look at how we see ourselves, how we think about ourselves, and how we speak to ourselves.

As you being this journey, trust and believe: *Philippians 1:6: Being confident of this very thing, that he who has begun a good work in you will complete it until the day of Jesus Christ.* When we decide to start, God is a promise keeper and He will do what he said, He would do. I encourage you to take your power and do the work. Girl, take your power and become self-aware of the is-ness of you, remember no one knows you better than you.

Remember, our goal together is for you to decide your WHY for this transformation journey. Take your time, feel where you are, breathe, and focus on the present. Also, quiet the inner critic. The cost of inaccurate thinking creates unnecessary suffering in your life. It will lead you to waste a lot of time and energy.

Girl, get up and walk in your full authority! Get up and try again! Get up and take a chance again! Get up and see yourself through a new lens! Girl, get up! You are not what you did! Girl get up! You are not just your title nor the roll you play! Girl get up! You are powerful, thought provoking, creative, amazing, and transformed!

GIRL! LET'S START TODAY!

Let's DIG DEEP!

Opening Assignments:

Write out your thoughts of transformation.

_____
_____
_____
_____

How do you see yourself transforming?

_____
_____
_____
_____

Why is it important for you to start your transformation journey?

_____
_____
_____
_____

What date will you start your journey? _____

Why do you feel this is the time to start your transformation?

_____
_____
_____
_____

What emotion do you experience when you think of transformation?

_____
_____
_____
_____

What three words describe you best?

_____
_____
_____
_____

Why have you chosen those words?

_____
_____
_____
_____

How do you live each word daily?

_____
_____
_____
_____

Write your Biography not your obituary

Write a biography of 500 words in 20 minutes. This will allow you to type very easily and care less about what you are going to include. Allowing yourself to define what your brain thinks is most important when it comes to identifying who you are.

_____
_____
_____
_____
_____
_____
_____
_____
_____
_____
_____
_____
_____
_____
_____
_____
_____
_____
_____

Create Your Positive I AM Statements

Creating your positive I AM statements is a very easy process. Get a blank sheet of paper and a good pen, stand in front of a mirror, look yourself in the eye and say "I AM . . . . ." Write it down. Look at yourself again, and say "I AM . . . . . " Write it down. Repeat this process for at least 15 minutes. Set the list aside for at least 24 hours. Then pick it up again and review your list. If there is anything negative or limiting at all, cross it out furiously. I mean, really put some angry, disgusted fervor in removing it from your list. Make sure it is completely blacked out so that you cannot read it anymore.

I AM......	I AM......
I AM.....	I AM......
I AM.....	I AM......
I AM.....	I AM......
I AM.....	I AM......
I AM.....	I AM......
I AM.....	I AM......
I AM.....	I AM......

How to Use Your Positive I AM Statements

Now that you have a list of positive I AM statements, you need to use them. Read them out loud. Say them with enthusiasm! Jump for joy if you feel it! Pump your arms like Rocky at the top of the steps! Other positive I AM statements will start to come to you. WRITE THEM DOWN! Repeat your list as many times as it feels right. Do this exercise 2 or 3 times a day and you will notice that your mood improves, your patience with others increases, your breathing deepens, and you will start to feel lighter and more energized.

The Search for WHY?

People who have a sense of purpose are often seen as being unstoppable. They are capable of shaping their lives their way. When you become laser-focused on your goals, you will have no question as to why you got up each day and what you must accomplish.

Simon Sinek, author of the book, *Find Your Why: A Practical Guide for Finding Purpose for You and Your Team,* writes "that it is only when you understand your "why" (or your purpose) that you will be more capable of pursuing the things that give you fulfillment. It will serve as your point of reference for all your actions and decisions from this moment on, allowing you to measure your progress and know when you have met your goals."

What is your WHY?

What are your **GOALS?:**

Spiritual?

Why? _____

Why? _____

Why? _____

Career/Business?

Why? _____

Why? _____

Why? _____

Personal?

Why? _____

Why? _____

Why? _____

VALUES EXERCISE ADAPTED FROM TAPROOT
(http://www.taproot.com/archives/37771)

Assignment #1. Determine your core values. From the list below, choose and write down every core value that resonates with you. Do not overthink your selections. As you read through the list, simply write down the words that feel like a core value to you personally. If you think of a value you possess that is not on the list, be sure to write it down.

Abundance	Acceptance	Accountability
Achievement	Advancement	Adventure
Advocacy	Ambition	Appreciation
Attractiveness	Autonomy	Balance
Being the Best	Benevolence	Boldness
Brilliance	Calmness	Caring
Challenge	Charity	Cheerfulness
Cleverness	Community	Commitment
Compassion	Cooperation	Consistency
Contribution	Creativity	Credibility
Curiosity	Daring	Decisiveness
Dedication	Dependability	Diversity
Empathy	Encouragement	Enthusiasm
Ethics	Excellence	Expressiveness
Fairness	Family	Friendships
Flexibility	Freedom	Fun
Generosity	Grace	Growth
Flexibility	Happiness	Health
Honesty	Humility	Humor
Inclusiveness	Independence	Individuality

Innovation	Inspiration	Intelligence
Intuition	Joy	Kindness
Knowledge	Leadership	Learning
Love	Loyalty	Making a Difference
Stability	Professionalism	Quality
Recognition	Risk Taking	Safety
Service	Spirituality	Security
Peace	Perfection	Playfulness
Popularity	Power	Preparedness
Proactivity	Professionalism	Punctuality
Recognition	Relationships	Reliability
Resilience	Resourcefulness	Responsibility
Responsiveness	Self-Control	Selflessness
Simplicity	Success	Teamwork
Thankfulness	Thoughtfulness	Traditionalism
Trustworthiness	Understanding	Uniqueness
Usefulness	Versatility	Vision
Warmth	Wealth	Well-Being
Wisdom	Zeal	

Assignment #2. Create the core values from the above list that stands out to you. Group them in a way that makes sense to you, personally.

Assignment #3. Choose fifteen words from the above grouping that speaks to you the greatest, that feels natural to you. Again, do not overthink. There are no right or wrong answers. You are defining the answer that is right for you.

1.	2.	3.
4.	5.	6.
7.	8.	9.
10.	11.	12.
13.	14.	15.

Assignment #4. Now look over the above values and select six core values that stand out the greatest?

1.	3.	5.
2.	4.	6.

What would you want to say to yourself 1 year in the future?

_____
_____
_____
_____

What would you want to say to yourself 3 years in the future?

_____
_____
_____
_____

What would you want to say to yourself 5 years in the future?

_____
_____
_____
_____

What would you want to say to yourself 10 years in the future?

_____
_____
_____
_____

It's My Life ~ WEEK ONE

Scripture to Memorize

May God himself, the God of peace, sanctify you through and through. May your whole spirit, soul and body be kept blameless at the coming of our Lord Jesus Christ. The one who calls you is faithful, and he will do it. I Thessalonians 5:23-24 (NIV)

Weekly Prayer

Dear Lord, I come before you boldly to obtain grace and mercy. Lord I ask for your guidance as I start my *transformation* work. I ask forgiveness of all the negative and harmful words I have spoken about myself. Forgive me for neglecting myself. So often I have failed to cultivate my spirit by not spending time with you. Lord I forget those things that are behind me, including all of my personal short comings. Lord, I press towards the mark of the high calling in Christ Jesus. Lord, I thank you for your love. Help me to love myself as you love me. Amen.

Share My Heart Prayer (Write a prayer from your heart to God.)

_____

_____

_____

_____

Weekly Affirmation

I am cooperating with God as He transforms me day by day.

Write out the above affirmation on an index card and read it over and over every morning.

Personal Affirmation

Create your own affirmation for this week that speaks life to you.

_____
_____
_____
_____

What are my Intentions for this week?

Write out what you want to accomplish for this week. No matter how large or small it may be, be intentional.

_____
_____
_____
_____

What steps will you take to manifest your accomplishments THIS week?

_____
_____
_____
_____

Every Morning

Every morning, write three things you are grateful for. (Write something different every day – no matter how small it may seem to you)

Monday	Tuesday	Wednesday	Thursday	Friday	Saturday	Sunday

My weekly schedule will look like this!

Week of: _____

5:00am _____

5:30am _____

6:00am _____

6:30am _____

7:00am _____

7:30am _____

8:00am _____

8:30am _____

9:00am _____

9:30am _____

10:00am _____

10:30am _____

11:00am _____

11:30am _____

12noon _____

12:30pm _____

1:00pm _____

1:30pm _____

2:00pm _____

2:30pm _____

3:00pm _____

3:30pm _____

4:00pm _____

4:30pm _____

5:00pm _____

5:30pm _____

6:00pm _____

6:30pm _____

7:00pm _____

7:30pm _____

8:00pm _____

8:30pm _____

9:00pm _____

9:30pm _____

10:00pm _____

10:30pm _____

11:00pm _____

11:30pm _____

12:00am _____

12:30am _____

1:00am _____

1:30am _____

2:00am _____

2:30am _____

3:00am _____

3:30am _____

4:00am _____

4:30am _____

I will take ownership of my ATTITUDE. How will I do it?

_____
_____
_____
_____

Detox your thinking. I admit I have stinking thinking in the area(s) of:

_____
_____
_____
_____

Write one of your core values.

_____
_____
_____
_____

How is this core value showing up in your life?

_____
_____
_____
_____

What is one priority for this week and what action will you take to complete it?

_____
_____
_____
_____

What self-care will I apply this week?

_____
_____
_____
_____

I am the perfect age today.

What would I say to my younger self on today?

_____
_____
_____
_____

What is your I AM statement for this week?

I AM_____

DAY ONE QUESTION

Life is filled with obstacles that are outside of our control. We need to look deeper at what we have control over, that is our thoughts. Romans 12:2 And be not conformed to this world: but be ye transformed by the renewing of your mind, and perfect, will of God.
We must understand, negative thoughts manifest and causes visible and invisible damage.

What is your inner dialogue like?
What are your beliefs about yourself?
What do you say to yourself that you would not say out loud in front of others?

List the conversations you have with yourself.

1. _____
2. _____
3. _____
4. _____
5. _____
6. _____
7. _____
8. _____

Label each either (P) for POSITIVE or (N) for NEGATIVE. Be honest.

What action will you take to change the negative?

DAY TWO QUESTION

The Oxford Dictionary states:
CHANGE- Make or become different, take or use another instead of, the act or instance of making or become different
Change requires you to make a conscious choice. Colossians 3:10 And have put on the new man, which is renewed in knowledge after the image of Him that created him.

What areas in my life do I need to change?
Why is this change necessary?
What steps are you willing to take towards change?

_____
_____
_____
_____
_____
_____
_____
_____
_____
_____
_____
_____
_____

DAY THREE QUESTION

Do you believe in yourself? If yes, how do you show it?
If no, what will you do to start the journey?
What do you believe happened that caused self-doubt?

_____
_____
_____
_____
_____
_____
_____
_____
_____
_____
_____
_____
_____
_____
_____
_____
_____
_____
_____

DAY FOUR QUESTION

What are your impulses?
How are they controlling you?

DAY FIVE QUESTION

How do you respond to your feelings? (fear, pride, stress, anxiety, hope)

DAY SIX QUESTION

How do you self-examine?

DAY SEVEN QUESTION

One way I will rest today?

Go to a quiet place and follow the breathing exercise below.

Pursed Lip Breathing Technique

This simple breathing technique makes you slow down your pace of breathing by having you apply deliberate effort in each breath. You can practice pursed lip breathing at any time. It may be especially useful during activities such as bending, lifting or stair climbing. To learn this breathing technique, practice 4 to 5 times a day.

How to do it:

1. Relax your neck and shoulders.
2. Keeping your mouth closed, inhale slowly through your nose for 2 counts.
3. Pucker or purse your lips as though you were going to whistle.
4. Exhale slowly by blowing air through your pursed lips for a count of 4.

CONCLUSION OF WEEK ONE

I Feel……

_____
_____
_____
_____
_____
_____

Why?

_____
_____
_____
_____
_____
_____

I am Grateful for……

_____
_____
_____
_____
_____
_____

WEEK ONE NOTES

WHAT I LEARNED ABOUT MYSELF

I don't have to start over; I simply make the choice to begin where I last ended.

-- Zareta S. Greene

"It's not about perfect. It's about effort. And when you implement that effort into your life. Every single day, that's where transformation happens. That's how change occurs. Keep going. Remember why you started."

— Anonymous

It's My Life ~ WEEK TWO

Scripture to Memorize

Therefore, when you prepare your minds for action; by being self-controlled, put your hope completely in the grace that will be brought to you at the revelation of Jesus Christ. As obedient children, do not be conformed to the former desires you used to conform to in your ignorance, but as the one who called you is holy, you yourselves be holy in all your conduct, for it is written "You will be holy, because I am holy. 1 Peter 1:13-16 (LEB)

Weekly Prayer

Dear Lord, I come before you boldly to obtain peace. Lord, you are peace, you don't just give it. You are peace that passes all understanding. Lord, guide me into your presence so that I may hear you and follow you wherever you lead me. For in my inner being, I delight in you. Your word says, *This book of law shall not depart out of thy mouth, but thou shalt mediate therein day and night, that thou mayest observe to do according to all that is written therein: for then thou shalt make thy way prosperous, and then thou shalt have good success.* Thank you, Jesus, for good success! Thank you, Jesus, for direction. I agree with you Lord that you will make my way plain. Amen.

Share my Heart Prayer (Write a prayer from your heart to God.)

_____

_____

_____

_____

Weekly Affirmation

All I have to do is listen and God will show me which way to go.

Write the above affirmation on an index card and read it over and over every morning.

Personal Affirmation

Create your own affirmation for this week that speaks life to you.

_____
_____
_____
_____

What are my intentions for this week?

Write out what you want to accomplish for this week. No matter how large or small it may be, be intentional.

_____
_____
_____
_____

What steps will you take to manifest your accomplishments THIS week?

_____
_____
_____
_____

Every Morning

Every morning, write three things you are grateful for. (Write something different every day-no matter how small it may seem to you).

Sunday	Monday	Tuesday	Wednesday	Thursday	Friday	Saturday

My weekly schedule will look like this!

Week of: _____

5:00am _____

5:30am _____

6:00am _____

6:30am _____

7:00am _____

7:30am _____

8:00am _____

8:30am _____

9:00am _____

9:30am _____

10:00am _____

10:30am _____

11:00am _____

11:30am _____

12noon _____

12:30pm _____

1:00pm _____

1:30pm _____

2:00pm _____

2:30pm _____

3:00pm _____

3:30pm _____

4:00pm _____

4:30pm _____

5:00pm _____

5:30pm _____

6:00pm _____

6:30pm _____

7:00pm _____

7:30pm _____

8:00pm _____

8:30pm _____

9:00pm _____

9:30pm _____

10:00pm _____

10:30pm _____

11:00pm _____

11:30pm _____

12:00am _____

12:30am _____

1:00am _____

1:30am _____

2:00am _____

2:30am _____

3:00am _____

3:30am _____

4:00am _____

4:30am _____

I will take ownership of my ATTITUDE. How will I do it?

_____
_____
_____
_____

Detox from self-comparison: What does that look like to you?

_____
_____
_____
_____

Write one of your core values.

_____
_____
_____
_____

How is this core value showing up in your life?

_____
_____
_____
_____

What is one priority for this week and what action will you take to complete it?

_____

_____

_____

_____

What self-care will I apply this week?

_____

_____

_____

_____

Assignment #1. Write a handwritten letter to a person you are particularly grateful to have in your life. Be detailed. Express all the wonderful qualities about this person and how they personally have affected your life for the better. Mail it to them.

What's your **I AM** statement for this week?

I AM _____

DAY EIGHT QUESTION

What impact do you want to have on other people's lives or in the world?

DAY NINE QUESTION

Whom can you count on for support?
Please name each person and how they are supportive to you.

DAY TEN QUESTION

What is your dream?
Is that dream realistic? If no, why not?
What do you need to do to make it a reality? If Yes, what steps will you take towards it?

_____
_____
_____
_____
_____
_____
_____
_____
_____
_____
_____
_____
_____
_____
_____
_____

DAY ELEVEN QUESTION

What challenge excites you the most in your life right now?

DAY TWELVE QUESTION

Do you believe that you can love what you do and make money doing it? If so, how?

DAY THIRTEEN QUESTION

Do you feel confident that you are exceptional at something?
What is it?
What makes it exceptional?

DAY FOURTEEN QUESTION

What do you want: more joy or more power? Why or why not?

CONCLUSION OF WEEK TWO

I Feel……

_____
_____
_____
_____
_____
_____

Why?

_____
_____
_____
_____
_____
_____

I am Grateful for……

_____
_____
_____
_____
_____
_____
_____

WEEK TWO NOTES

WHAT I LEARNED ABOUT MYSELF

I am a Woman

Phenomenally.

Phenomenal Woman,

That's me.

-- Maya Angelou

Change can be hard. It requires no extra effort to settle for the same old thing. Auto-pilot keeps us locked into past patterns. But transforming your life? That requires courage, commitment, and effort. It's tempting to stay camped in the zone of That's-Just-How-It-Is. But to get to the really good stuff in life, you have to be willing to become an explorer and adventurer.

– John Mark Green

It's My Life ~ WEEK THREE

Scripture to Memorize

Do you not know that your body is a temple of the (the very sanctuary) of the Holy Spirit, who lives within you, whom you have received (as a gift) from God? You are not your own, you were bought with a price (purchased with a preciousness and paid for, made His own) So then, honor God and bring glory to Him in your body. 1 Corinthians 6:19-20 AMPC

Weekly Prayer

Father, in the name of Jesus, allow nothing to separate me from you. Lord, teach me how to choose only your ways and allow each of my steps to lead me closer to you. I will walk in Your word and not my feelings. Lord, help me to keep my heart pure and undivided. Lord, your word tells me great is Your love towards me. I know Your love for me is not based on my performance, you are my loving father, amazing savior. Allow Your will to be walked out in me. I declare and decree I am precious to God and He will take care of me. I declare and decree God has filled my life with good things. I can trust Him to satisfy me. Psalms 103:1-5

Share my Heart Prayer (Write a prayer from your heart to God.)

_____
_____
_____
_____

Weekly Affirmation

I am committed to transform my body, my mind and my soul according to God's desires for me.

Write out the above affirmation on an index card and read it over and over every morning.

Personal Affirmation

Create your own affirmation for this week, that speaks life to you.

_____
_____
_____
_____

What is my intention for this week?

_____
_____
_____
_____

Write out what you want to accomplish for this week. No matter how large or how small it may be, be intentional.

_____
_____
_____
_____

What steps will you take to manifest your accomplishments THIS week?

_____
_____
_____
_____

Every Morning

Every morning, write three things you are grateful for. (Write something different every day-no matter how small it may seem to you.)

Monday	Tuesday	Wednesday	Thursday	Friday	Saturday	Sunday

My weekly schedule will look like this!

Week of: _____

5:00am _____

5:30am _____

6:00am _____

6:30am _____

7:00am _____

7:30am _____

8:00am _____

8:30am _____

9:00am _____

9:30am _____

10:00am _____

10:30am _____

11:00am _____

11:30am _____

12noon _____

12:30pm _____

1:00pm _____

1:30pm _____

2:00pm _____

2:30pm _____

3:00pm _____

3:30pm _____

4:00pm _____

4:30pm _____

5:00pm _____

5:30pm _____

6:00pm _____

6:30pm _____

7:00pm _____

7:30pm _____

8:00pm _____

8:30pm _____

9:00pm _____

9:30pm _____

10:00pm _____

10:30pm _____

11:00pm _____

11:30pm _____

12:00am _____

12:30am _____

1:00am _____

1:30am _____

2:00am _____

2:30am _____

3:00am _____

3:30am _____

4:00am _____

4:30am _____

I will take ownership of my SPEECH.

Detox your negative speech. I will reframe from saying anything negative.

What does that look like to you?

_____
_____
_____
_____

Write one of your core values.

_____
_____
_____
_____

How is this core value showing up in your life?

_____
_____
_____
_____

What is one priority for this week and what action will you take to complete it?

_____
_____
_____
_____

What self-care will I apply this week?

_____

_____

_____

_____

I am free. What are you free from?

_____

_____

_____

_____

What is your I AM statement for this week?

I AM _____

DAY FIFTEEN QUESTION

Do you exercise, eat healthy, and take care of yourself?
If not, why not? If not, challenge your reasons.
If yes, what is your schedule and what is your level of commitment?

DAY SIXTEEN QUESTION

Whom do you admire most? Why?
List the characteristics you admire about that person.

DAY SEVENTEEN QUESTION

What is your #1 confidence barrier?

DAY EIGHTEEN QUESTION

What can you do to work on that barrier?

DAY NINETEEN QUESTION

What is your greatest fear?

DAY TWENTY QUESTION

What advice would you give yourself today about where you are in your life and where you want to go?

DAY TWENTY-ONE QUESTION

When was the last time you told yourself "I love you?"

CONCLUSION OF WEEK THREE

I Feel……

_____
_____
_____
_____
_____
_____

Why?

_____
_____
_____
_____
_____
_____

I am Grateful for……

_____
_____
_____
_____
_____
_____

WEEK THREE NOTES

WHAT I LEARNED ABOUT MYSELF

_____
_____
_____
_____
_____
_____
_____
_____
_____
_____
_____
_____
_____
_____
_____
_____
_____
_____

There is no limit to what we,

as women, can accomplish.

-- Michelle Obama

Transformation is a process, and as life happens there are tons of ups and downs. It's a journey of discovery — there are moments on mountaintops and moments in deep valleys of despair.

— Rick Warren

It's My Life ~ WEEK FOUR

Scripture to Memorize

I sought the Lord, and he answered me; he delivered me from all my fears. Those who look to him are radiant; their faces are never covered with shame. Psalm 34:4-5 (NIV)

Weekly Prayer

Father, my God and my Savior. When I called out to God, He answered me He tells me things I wouldn't know otherwise. Jeremiah 33:3 Call to Me and I will answer you, and tell you and even show you, great and mighty things, things which have been confined and hidden, which you do not know and understand and cannot distinguish. Today is a new day, a new chance for a new start. Yesterday is gone with all of my short comings and failures. In this new mercy Lord, I will seize the opportunity to walk in my spiritual inheritance. I will set my foot down on every promise in You God. I declare and decree, I am not destined for stumbling or destruction. I have a noble purpose and a hope, according to 1 Peter 2:9, But you are a chosen race, a royal priesthood, a consecrated nation, a special people for God's own possession so that you may proclaim the excellencies the wonderful deeds and virtues and perfections of Him who called you out of darkness into His marvelous light. Amen and Amen.

Share my Heart Prayer (Write a prayer from your heart to God.)

_____

_____

_____

_____

Weekly Affirmation

Today is a new mercy and I live in the blessings of the Lord.

Write out the above affirmation on an index card and read it over and over every morning.

Personal Affirmation

Create your own affirmation for this week that speaks life to you.

_____
_____
_____
_____

What is your intention for this week?

Write out what you want to accomplish for this week. No matter how large or how small it may be, be intentional.

_____
_____
_____
_____

What steps will you take to manifest your accomplishments THIS week?

_____
_____
_____
_____

Every Morning

Every morning, write three things you are grateful for, (please pick something different every day, no matter how small it may seem).

Monday	Tuesday	Wednesday	Thursday	Friday	Saturday	Sunday

My weekly schedule will look like this!

Week of: _____

5:00am _____

5:30am _____

6:00am _____

6:30am _____

7:00am _____

7:30am _____

8:00am _____

8:30am _____

9:00am _____

9:30am _____

10:00am _____

10:30am _____

11:00am _____

11:30am _____

12noon _____

12:30pm _____

1:00pm _____

1:30pm _____

2:00pm _____

2:30pm _____

3:00pm _____

3:30pm _____

4:00pm _____

4:30pm _____

5:00pm _____

5:30pm _____

6:00pm _____

6:30pm _____

7:00pm _____

7:30pm _____

8:00pm _____

8:30pm _____

9:00pm _____

9:30pm _____

10:00pm _____

10:30pm _____

11:00pm _____

11:30pm _____

12:00am _____

12:30am _____

1:00am _____

1:30am _____

2:00am _____

2:30am _____

3:00am _____

3:30am _____

4:00am _____

4:30am _____

I will take ownership of my THOUGHTS:

Detox from your clutter! What area(s) in your life do you need to declutter?

What does that look like to you?

_____
_____
_____
_____

Write one of your core values.

_____
_____
_____
_____

How is this core value showing up in your life?

_____
_____
_____
_____

What is one priority for this week and what action will you take to complete it?

_____
_____
_____
_____

What self-care will I apply this week?

I love who I am. What you do love about yourself?

In what ways are you loving yourself?

_____

_____

_____

_____

What is your I AM statement for this week?

I AM _____

DAY TWENTY-TWO QUESTION

Am I a better person today than I was yesterday?

DAY TWENTY-THREE QUESTION

Are my actions guided by love, or by fear?

DAY TWENTY-FOUR QUESTION

Am I a good example for those around me?

DAY TWENTY-FIVE QUESTION

Is the life that I am living the life I want to be living?

DAY TWENTY-SIX QUESTION

What would I do with my life if I knew there were no limits?

DAY TWENTY-SEVEN QUESTION

Do the people I surround myself with add any value to my life?
Be real and examine each person that you surround yourself with. What value do they bring?

DAY TWENTY-EIGHT QUESTION

Am I a Human Being or a Human Doing?

CONCLUSION OF WEEK FOUR

I Feel......

_____

_____

_____

_____

_____

Why?

_____

_____

_____

_____

_____

I am Grateful for......

_____

_____

_____

_____

_____

WEEK FOUR NOTES

WHAT I LEARNED ABOUT MYSELF?

Words have power. TV has power.

My pen has power.

- Shonda Rhimes

You can't have a physical transformation until you have a spiritual transformation.

— Cory Booker

It's My Life ~ WEEK FIVE

Scripture to Memorize

But they that wait upon the Lord shall renew their strength; they shall mount up with wings as eagles; they shall run, and not be weary; and they shall walk, and not faint. Isaiah 40:31 (KJV)

Weekly Prayer

Father God we speak your word this morning. You told us in Isaiah 40:29: He gives strength to the weary and increases the power of the weak. Lord, Thank You for strength to get up and become what You called me to be. Lord thank you, those who hope in the Lord will renew their strength. They will soar on wings eagles; they will run and not grow weary; they will walk and not faint. Father, we thank You for saying to me "my grace is sufficient for you, for my power is made perfect in weakness. Lord, we declare and decree I am strong and persistent; I decree and decree I am the head and not the tail, above and not beneath. I agree with God.

Share my Heart Prayer (Write a prayer from your heart to God.)

_____

_____

_____

_____

Weekly Affirmation

I am fully aware of myself and I give myself permission to live.

Write out the above affirmation on an index card and read it over and over every morning.

Personal Affirmation

Create your own affirmation for this week, that speaks life to you.

_____
_____
_____
_____

What is my intention for this week?

Write out what you want to accomplish for this week. No matter how large or how small it may be, be intentional.

_____
_____
_____
_____

What steps will you take to manifest your accomplishments THIS week?

_____
_____
_____
_____

Every Morning

Every morning, write three things you are grateful for. Write something different every day – no matter how small it may seem to you.

Monday	Tuesday	Wednesday	Thursday	Friday	Saturday	Sunday

My weekly schedule will look like this!

Week of: _____

5:00am _____

5:30am _____

6:00am _____

6:30am _____

7:00am _____

7:30am _____

8:00am _____

8:30am _____

9:00am _____

9:30am _____

10:00am _____

10:30am _____

11:00am _____

11:30am _____

12noon _____

12:30pm _____

1:00pm _____

1:30pm _____

2:00pm _____

2:30pm _____

3:00pm _____

3:30pm _____

4:00pm _____

4:30pm _____

5:00pm _____

5:30pm _____

6:00pm _____

6:30pm _____

7:00pm _____

7:30pm _____

8:00pm _____

8:30pm _____

9:00pm _____

9:30pm _____

10:00pm _____

10:30pm _____

11:00pm _____

11:30pm _____

12:00am _____

12:30am _____

1:00am _____

1:30am _____

2:00am _____

2:30am _____

3:00am _____

3:30am _____

4:00am _____

4:30am _____

I will take ownership of my Finances?

Detox your finances! I will take time to record all my bills and create a budget.

_____
_____
_____
_____

Write one of your core values.

_____
_____
_____
_____

How is this core value showing up in your life?

_____
_____
_____
_____

What is one priority for this week and what action will you take to complete it?

_____
_____
_____
_____

What form of self-care will I apply this week?

I forgive the past. A large part of the work of forgiveness involves changing your own personal story — not the reality, just your interpretation of it.

How were you hurt? How has it affected you even today?

How does it hold you back from enjoying life, trusting others, and opening yourself up to new experiences?

_____
_____
_____
_____

What is your I AM statement for this week?

I AM _____

DAY TWENTY-NINE QUESTION

What would I do differently if I knew nobody would judge me?

DAY THIRTY QUESTION

Do I treat <u>myself</u> with the love and respect I truly deserve?

DAY THIRTY-ONE QUESTION

What is one thing I could start doing today to improve the quality of my life?

DAY THIRTY-TWO QUESTION

When was the last time I heard the words 'I love you'?

DAY THIRTY-THREE QUESTION

When was the last time I did something nice for myself?

DAY THIRTY-FOUR QUESTION

When was the last time I learned something new?
What was it?

DAY THIRTY-FIVE QUESTION

When was the last time I did something fun?

CONCLUSION OF WEEK FIVE

I Feel……

Why?

I am Grateful for……

WEEK FIVE NOTES

WHAT I LEARNED ABOUT MYSELF?

We need to reshape our own perception of how we view ourselves. We have to step up as women and take the lead.

— Beyoncé

Nothing gets transformed in your life until your mind is transformed.

— Ifeanyi Enoch Onuoha

It's My Life ~ WEEK SIX

Scripture to Memorize

Come unto Me, all ye that labour and are heavy laden, and I will give you rest. Take My yoke upon you, and learn of me; for I am meek and lowly in heart: and ye shall find rest unto my souls. Matthew 11:28-29 (KJV)

Weekly Prayer

Dear Lord I am weary; my mind is full of emotions and my life feels overwhelming. I feel I have accomplished little. I call on You to send the peace. Help me not to miss Your divine appointment and reveal to me the things I should give focus. Lord, when anxiety, fear, and turmoil arrives, Lord silence the voices of doubt and speak Your word of truth. According to *Psalms 107:20 You sent Your word, and delivered them from all their destructions. Lord, bring productivity and contentment out of the disappointment. Peace and comfort, settle me in Your truth, power and authority. I choose to enter Your secret place according to Your word; I sought the Lord and You heard me and delivered me from all of my fears.*

Share my Heart Prayer (Write a prayer from your heart to God.)

_____

_____

_____

_____

Weekly Affirmation

I reject negative, thinking, and speaking. I take my mind back and product positive thinking, and speaking.

Write out the above affirmation on an index card and read it over and over every morning.

Personal Affirmation

Create your own affirmation for this week, that speaks life to you.

_____
_____
_____
_____

What is your intention for this week?

Write out what you want to accomplish for this week. No matter how large or how small it may be, be intentional.

_____
_____
_____
_____

What steps will you take to manifest your accomplishments THIS week?

_____
_____
_____
_____

Every Morning

Every morning, write three things you are grateful for. Write something different every day, no matter how small it may seem to you.

Monday	Tuesday	Wednesday	Thursday	Friday	Saturday	Sunday

My weekly schedule will look like this!

Week of: _____

5:00am _____

5:30am _____

6:00am _____

6:30am _____

7:00am _____

7:30am _____

8:00am _____

8:30am _____

9:00am _____

9:30am _____

10:00am _____

10:30am _____

11:00am _____

11:30am _____

12noon _____

12:30pm _____

1:00pm _____

1:30pm _____

2:00pm _____

2:30pm _____

3:00pm _____

3:30pm _____

4:00pm _____

4:30pm _____

5:00pm _____

5:30pm _____

6:00pm _____

6:30pm _____

7:00pm _____

7:30pm _____

8:00pm _____

8:30pm _____

9:00pm _____

9:30pm _____

10:00pm _____

10:30pm _____

11:00pm _____

11:30pm _____

12:00am _____

12:30am _____

1:00am _____

1:30am _____

2:00am _____

2:30am _____

3:00am _____

3:30am _____

4:00am _____

4:30am _____

I will take ownership of my HEALTH.

Detox from lack of rest - *Am I getting enough rest and am I getting quality rest?*

What does that look like to you?

_____
_____
_____
_____

Write one of your core values.

_____
_____
_____
_____

How is this core value showing up in your life?

_____
_____
_____
_____

What is one priority for this week and what action will you take to complete it?

_____
_____
_____
_____

What self-care will I apply this week?

Forgive yourself, you are worth it!

I did then what I knew to do. Now that I know better, I do better. – Maya Angelou

Self-forgiveness is the first step in freeing yourself from self-judgment.

The important questions are:
- Did you learn from your regrets and past actions and choices?
- Are you using those choices and even errors in judgments as springboards to having more insight and maturity now?
- Are you currently making decisions that you are happy with based on the wisdom you earned?

_____

_____

_____

_____

What is your I AM statement for this week?

I AM _____

DAY #36 QUESTION

Am I a source of inspiration for my friends and family?

DAY #37 QUESTION

What does the child inside of me long for?

DAY #38 QUESTION

What is one thing <u>right now</u> that you are totally sure of?

DAY #39 QUESTION

Are you willing to take a risk with your career and your comfort zone?

DAY #40 QUESTION

When was the last time you did something that scared you?

DAY #41 QUESTION

What new behavior would help you achieve your goals?

DAY #42 QUESTION

Do you feel confident most of the time or do you struggle a lot?

CONCLUSION OF WEEK SIX

I Feel......

_____
_____
_____
_____
_____

Why?

_____
_____
_____
_____
_____

I am Grateful for......

_____
_____
_____
_____
_____
_____

WEEK SIX NOTES

WHAT I LEARNED ABOUT MYSELF?

You are one decision away from living the life of your dreams! If you don't like what's going on in your life, you can make the decision to change. When you change, everything else adjusts to accommodate that change!

- Dr. Cindy Trimm

As the caterpillar undergoes transformation within the cocoon before emerging as a butterfly; likewise, life experiences shape character.

– Lorna Jackie

It's My Life ~ WEEK SEVEN

Scripture to Memorize

Do you not know that in a race all the runners run, but only one gets the prize? Run in such a way as to get the prize. Everyone who competes in the games goes into strict training. They do it to get a crown that will not last; but we do it to get a crown that will last forever. I Corinthians 9:24-25 BNT

Weekly Prayer

Dear Lord, You created me for a purpose. Enable and equip me I pray, to fulfill the plan and purpose that You have for me to do and I ask that You would use each gift and every talent that You have graciously given to me. *Father for all the promises of God in him are yea, and in him Amen, unto the glory of God by us. II Corinthians 1:20. King James Version*

Help me to fulfill the election and calling. *For promotion cometh neither from the east, nor the from the west, nor from the south. But God is the judge: He putteth down one, and setteth up another Psalm75:6-7 King James Version.* You placed in my heart from birth You would have me do in my life and may I be obedient to Your voice as I seek to carry out Your purpose for my life. May I rejoice evermore and pray without ceasing.

Share my Heart Prayer (Write a prayer from your heart to God.)

_____

_____

_____

_____

Weekly Affirmation

I am full of wisdom; nothing I face today will hinder me.

Write out the above affirmation on an index card and read it over and over every morning.

Personal Affirmation

Create your own affirmation for this week that speaks life to you.

_____
_____
_____
_____

What is my intention for this week?

Write out what you want to accomplish for this week. No matter how large or how small it may be, be intentional.

_____
_____
_____
_____

What steps will you take to manifest your accomplishments THIS week?

_____
_____
_____
_____

Every Morning

Every morning, write three things you are grateful for. Write something different every day, no matter how small it may seem to you.

Sunday	Monday	Tuesday	Wednesday	Thursday	Friday	Saturday

My weekly schedule will look like this!

Week of: _____

5:00am _____

5:30am _____

6:00am _____

6:30am _____

7:00am _____

7:30am _____

8:00am _____

8:30am _____

9:00am _____

9:30am _____

10:00am _____

10:30am _____

11:00am _____

11:30am _____

12noon _____

12:30pm _____

1:00pm _____

1:30pm _____

2:00pm _____

2:30pm _____

3:00pm _____

3:30pm _____

4:00pm _____

4:30pm _____

5:00pm _____

5:30pm _____

6:00pm _____

6:30pm _____

7:00pm _____

7:30pm _____

8:00pm _____

8:30pm _____

9:00pm _____

9:30pm _____

10:00pm _____

10:30pm _____

11:00pm _____

11:30pm _____

12:00am _____

12:30am _____

1:00am _____

1:30am _____

2:00am _____

2:30am _____

3:00am _____

3:30am _____

4:00am _____

4:30am _____

I will take ownership of my SPIRITUAL life.

Detox from toxic people. Who are they?

What are you willing to do to start your detox of toxic people?

_____
_____
_____
_____

Write one of your core values.

_____
_____
_____
_____

How is this core value showing up in your life?

_____
_____
_____
_____

What is one priority for this week and what action will you take to complete it?

_____
_____
_____
_____

What self-care will I apply this week?

I am Resourceful. List your resources.

_____

_____

_____

_____

What is your I AM statement for this week?

I AM_____

DAY FORTY-THREE QUESTION

How important is spirituality to your life now?

DAY FORTY-FOUR QUESTION

What experiences have shaped your spiritual life the most?

DAY FORTY-FIVE QUESTION

Was there ever a time you believed God for a major thing in life? If yes, what was it? How did you feel to believe God in that way?

_____
_____
_____
_____
_____
_____
_____
_____
_____
_____
_____
_____
_____
_____
_____
_____
_____
_____
_____
_____

DAY FORTY-SIX QUESTION

What study habits do I want to put in place to strengthen my spiritual life?

DAY FORTY-SEVEN QUESTION

Prayer does not change God, but it changes him who prays. - Soren Kierkegaard
When you read the above quote what does it tell you happens when you pray?

_____
_____
_____
_____
_____
_____
_____
_____
_____
_____
_____
_____
_____
_____
_____
_____
_____
_____
_____

DAY FORTY-EIGHT QUESTION

If you had a "do over" button,
what one event in your life would you like to have a second chance and why?
What would you do different?
What have you learned?

_____
_____
_____
_____
_____
_____
_____
_____
_____
_____
_____
_____
_____
_____
_____
_____

DAY FORTY-NINE QUESTION

If your life was a movie, what movie would it be?
What role do you play?

CONCLUSION OF WEEK SEVEN

I Feel……

_____
_____
_____
_____
_____
_____

Why?

_____
_____
_____
_____
_____
_____

I am Grateful for……

_____
_____
_____
_____
_____
_____

WEEK SEVEN NOTES

WHAT I LEARNED ABOUT MYSELF?

Transformation stems from a shift in perspective... it also means looking at the positives and negatives of one's life and seeing what treasures can be recovered from the rubble.

— Patricia Commins

To transform yourself, you don't need to do big things. Just do small things in big way. Transformation will follow you.

— Rahul Sinha

It's My Life ~ WEEK EIGHT

Scripture to Memorize

I know the plans I have for you,' says the Lord. 'They are plans for good and not for disaster, to give you a future and a hope. Jeremiah 29:11 New Living Translation

Weekly Prayer

Dear Lord, as I start this day, help me remember that I belong to You and my desire is to act accordingly. Lord, I trust You and know You will meet my every need. Keep my feet from stumbling and my mind from wandering into distractions that could steal precious time and energy from the most important things You have designed for me. I commit myself to seek first the kingdom and Your righteousness. I'm proud to be Your child, Lord. My eyes are fixed on You and Your might, acts of love, joy and peace, today is filled with the wonder of Your love, the freedom of Your Spirit, and the joy of knowing You. Amen

Share my Heart Prayer (Write a prayer from your heart to God.)

_____

_____

_____

_____

Weekly Affirmation

All I have to do is listen and God will show me which way to go.

Write out the above affirmation on an index card and read it over and over every morning.

Personal Affirmation

Create your own affirmation for this week that speaks life to you.

_____
_____
_____
_____

What is my intention for this week?

Write out what you want to accomplish for this week. No matter how large or how small it may be, be intentional.

_____
_____
_____
_____

What steps will you take to manifest your accomplishments THIS week?

_____
_____
_____
_____

Every Morning

Every morning, write three things you are grateful for. Write something different every day, no matter how small it may seem to you.

Sunday	Monday	Tuesday	Wednesday	Thursday	Friday	Saturday

My weekly schedule will look like this!

Week of: _____

5:00am _____

5:30am _____

6:00am _____

6:30am _____

7:00am _____

7:30am _____

8:00am _____

8:30am _____

9:00am _____

9:30am _____

10:00am _____

10:30am _____

11:00am _____

11:30am _____

12noon _____

12:30pm _____

1:00pm _____

1:30pm _____

2:00pm _____

2:30pm _____

3:00pm _____

3:30pm _____

4:00pm _____

4:30pm _____

5:00pm _____

5:30pm _____

6:00pm _____

6:30pm _____

7:00pm _____

7:30pm _____

8:00pm _____

8:30pm _____

9:00pm _____

9:30pm _____

10:00pm _____

10:30pm _____

11:00pm _____

11:30pm _____

12:00am _____

12:30am _____

1:00am _____

1:30am _____

2:00am _____

2:30am _____

3:00am _____

3:30am _____

4:00am _____

4:30am _____

I will take ownership of my FEELINGS.

Detox from your devices. Take a break from your devices. A detox from technology can do your mind wonders.

What does that look like to you?

_____
_____
_____
_____

Write one of your core values.

_____
_____
_____
_____

How is this core value showing up in your life?

_____
_____
_____
_____

What is one priority for this week and what action will you take to complete it?

_____
_____
_____
_____

What self-care will I apply this week?

I have the power within me to create the life I desire.

Honor your power to choose by choosing thoughts and actions that positively contribute to your life.

How have you taken your power back?

What is your I AM statement for this week?

I AM_____

DAY FIFTY QUESTION

Write briefly one thing in your life that is simple and one thing that is complex.

DAY FIFTY-ONE QUESTION

Is the life that I am living the life I want?
If no? why not? Write out in details the life you want to live.
Next to each, write out in detail the actions you need to take to make it become your life.

_____
_____
_____
_____
_____
_____
_____
_____
_____
_____
_____
_____
_____
_____
_____

DAY FIFTY-TWO QUESTION

Am I a happy person?
If no, what hinders your happiness?
If yes, what will make your happy?

DAY FIFTY-THREE QUESTION

List all the things you love about yourself.
if you find this question hard, ask someone close to you to tell you things they love about you. With their answers, ask yourself do you see those things and if not, why?

___

DAY FIFTY-FOUR QUESTION

Today celebrate yourself. Share with someone how you have daily created habits of learning yourself.

DAY FIFTY-FIVE QUESTION

What changes have you made? Why?
How do you feel on Day 55?
What's different from day one – to day Fifty-five?

DAY FIFTY-SIX QUESTION

How is the "public you" different from the "private you" and Why?

CONCLUSION OF WEEK EIGHT

I Feel......

_____
_____
_____
_____
_____

Why?

_____
_____
_____
_____
_____

I am Grateful for......

_____
_____
_____
_____
_____

WEEK EIGHT NOTES

WHAT I LEARNED ABOUT MYSELF?

When someone chooses to value herself over the things she can buy, true transformation begins.

— Suze Orman

When you find your definitions in God, you find the very purpose for which you were created. Put your hand into God's hand, know His absolutes, demonstrate His love, present His truth, and the message of redemption and transformation will take hold.

— Ravi Zacharias

It's My Life ~ WEEK NINE

Scripture to Memorize

But seek ye first the kingdom of God, and his righteousness; and all these things shall be added unto you. Take therefore no thought for the morrow: for the morrow shall take thought for the things of itself. Sufficient unto the day is the evil thereof. Matthew 6:33-34 (KJV)

Weekly Prayer

Heavenly Father, Your word says that if we lack wisdom, we should ask You, as we come into your presence with thanksgiving and rejoicing in all that you offer. Thank You that You have walked with me as I transformed, in my mind, spirit and body. Lord, allow Your wisdom to rule and govern all my decisions. Lord, order my footsteps and my thoughts. Cleanse me, refresh me and renew a right spirit in me that I may walk after your precepts. Amen.

Share my Heart Prayer (Write a prayer from your heart to God.)

_____

_____

_____

_____

Weekly Affirmation

I AM CONFIDENT IN MY TALENTS, STRENGTHS, GIFTS, AND ABILITIES.

Write out the above affirmation on an index card and read it over and over every morning.

Personal Affirmation

Create your own affirmation for this week, that speaks life to you.

_____

_____

_____

_____

What is my intention for this week?

_____

_____

_____

_____

Write out what you want to accomplish for this week. No matter how large or how small, be intentional.

_____

_____

_____

_____

What steps will you take to manifest your accomplishments THIS week?

_____

_____

_____

_____

Every Morning

Every morning, write three things you are grateful for. Write something different every day, no matter how small it may seem to you.

I'm grateful for three things I hear.
I'm grateful for three things I see.
I'm grateful for these three friends.
I'm grateful for these three family members.
I'm grateful for these three things in my home.

Sunday	Monday	Tuesday	Wednesday	Thursday	Friday	Saturday

My weekly schedule will look like this!

Week of: _____

5:00am _____

5:30am _____

6:00am _____

6:30am _____

7:00am _____

7:30am _____

8:00am _____

8:30am _____

9:00am _____

9:30am _____

10:00am _____

10:30am _____

11:00am _____

11:30am _____

12noon _____

12:30pm _____

1:00pm _____

1:30pm _____

2:00pm _____

2:30pm _____

3:00pm _____

3:30pm _____

4:00pm _____

4:30pm _____

5:00pm _____

5:30pm _____

6:00pm _____

6:30pm _____

7:00pm _____

7:30pm _____

8:00pm _____

8:30pm _____

9:00pm _____

9:30pm _____

10:00pm _____

10:30pm _____

11:00pm _____

11:30pm _____

12:00am _____

12:30am _____

1:00am _____

1:30am _____

2:00am _____

2:30am _____

3:00am _____

3:30am _____

4:00am _____

4:30am _____

I will take ownership of HABITS.

Detox from your carnal interaction.

Pay attention to your spiritual needs. Spiritual needs are something that ought not to be neglected. Whether you meditate, read scripture, pray, attend church, enjoy the beauty of nature, or something else, doing the things that uplift your spirit is important to your balance and wellbeing.

What does that look like to you?

_____
_____
_____
_____

Write one of your core values.

_____
_____
_____
_____

How is this core value showing up in your life?

_____
_____
_____
_____

What is one priority for this week and what action will you take to complete it?

_____
_____
_____
_____

What self-care will I apply this week? Finish each sentence

I do my best when _____

I struggle when _____

I am comfortable when _____

I feel stress when _____

I am courageous when _____

One of the most important things I learned was _____

I missed a great opportunity when _____

One of my favorite memories is_____

My toughest decisions involve _____

Being myself is hard because _____

I can be myself when _____

I wish I were more _____

I wish I could_____

I wish I would regularly_____

I wish I had _____

I wish I knew _____

I wish I felt _____

I wish I saw _____

I wish I thought_____

Life should be about _____

I am going to make my life about _____

Once you finish completing the sentences, you should have insight into who you really are and what is most important to you. Use your answers to inform your decisions about what goals you choose to strive toward, what you would like to do in the future, and what moves to make next.

What is your I AM statement for this week?

I AM_____

CELEBRATE YOURSELF!

You have come a long way and you have done well.

The process of transformation provides incredible opportunity for inner learnings, expansion and growth. You have discovered so much about yourself.

Write your story of transformation. What does transformation mean to you?

What steps you took to transform?

What changes have you made that makes you feel good today?

Assignment

Part 1: Write a list of twenty-five things you want to HAVE, DO or BE. Label next to each either an (H) for HAVE, (D) for DO, or (B) for BE.

1. _____
2. _____
3. _____
4. _____
5. _____
6. _____
7. _____
8. _____
9. _____
10. _____
11. _____
12. _____
13. _____
14. _____
15. _____
16. _____
17. _____
18. _____
19. _____
20. _____
21. _____
22. _____
23. _____
24. _____
25. _____

Part 2: Review your twenty-five things and list the top five in the categories below:

HAVE	DO	BE
1.	1.	1.
2.	2.	2.
3.	3.	3.
4.	4.	4.
5.	5.	5.

Why do you want to **HAVE** it?
_____

Why do you want to **HAVE** it?
_____

Why do you want to **HAVE** it?
_____

Why do you want to **HAVE** it?
_____

Why do you want to **HAVE** it?
_____

Why do you want to DO It?

_____

Why do you want to DO It?

_____

Why do you want to DO It?

_____

Why do you want to DO It?

_____

Why do you want to DO It?

_____

Why do you want to BE?

_____

Why do you want to BE?

_____

Why do you want to BE?

_____

Why do you want to BE?

_____

Why do you want to BE?

_____

Assignment

Write Morning Pages. This exercise comes from the book, *An Artist's Way*. (There are many iterations on the market.)

Writing Morning Pages is very useful to produce insights, calm anxieties, and resolve problems. As soon as you wake up, grab a piece of paper and write everything that comes to mind. Don't filter anything—you want to declutter your mind.

The recommendation is to compose three pages of stream-of-consciousness writing. Some people do more. Others set a time limit—15 to 20 minutes. Doing it in the morning is ideal. You want to let everything out before your mind gets busy and starts filtering things.

Writing Morning Pages can help you unblock emotions, discover ideas that were at an unconscious level, or identify areas for development. When you let your words flow, without any rational filter, you set your creativity free.

Morning Pages are private; you don't need to filter your words. Some people use them as a warm-up and then destroy them without checking what they wrote. Others use them as a source of inspiration or self-reflection. See what works for you.

This exercise is an unfiltered version of journaling—it will help you know yourself better and become more appreciative too.

Try to make this a habit in your life.

Every Morning

Every morning, write three things you are grateful for. Write something different every day, no matter how small it may seem to you.

- I'm grateful for three things I hear.
- I'm grateful for three things I see.
- I'm grateful for these three friends.
- I'm grateful for these three family members.
- I'm grateful for these three things in my home.

Sunday	Monday	Tuesday	Wednesday	Thursday	Friday	Saturday

When you live a life of gratitude, you will thrive and become sensitive and self-aware of all areas of your live.

Thank you for trusting the process and being present for your journey.

Elaine Tina Frazier

Elaine Tina Frazier is a woman of excellence who has been married to Billy Frazier for 36 years. She is a caring mother of three wonderful children, and grandmother to one grandson. She possesses countless talents, one of them as a great chef. She is a counselor who is sought after by souls both far and near. Billy and Tina teach a 6 to 12-week pre-marital class and post marital enrichment. They are known for their realness, honesty and ability to set the stage for a lasting relationship.

Elaine Tina believes that increased knowledge should be a way of life. She has attained the following degrees and credentials: an MBA from Metropolitan College of New York, Master's Degree in Counseling; a Bachelors of Biblical Counseling from Pillsbury College and Seminary; Bachelor's of Science in Business Administration, a Licensed Clinical Christian Counselor, Domestic Violence Counselor, a Certified New York City Courts Anger Management Facilitator and Grief Counseling, a United Chaplain for the State of New York. She is also certified in Couple Communications, Family Dynamics, Prepare and Enrich, Pre-marriage, Marriage, Family and Family Development, Self-Image Counselor. She is a Certified Masters Life Coach and Niche Coach, Happiness, Goal Setting, Life Purpose, Transformation Life Coach and Certified Relationship Workshop Facilitator.

Elaine Tina's love for women and their advancement prompted her to establish and facilitate a program, 90 Days to Becoming the Woman I Want to Be. The program consists of workshops with a twist. Elaine Tina has helped hundreds of women to walk in their destined place and live a healthier, fulfilled life.

Elaine Tina is the CEO and Founder of two non-profit organizations: a faith-based organization, Visions Life Counseling Services, Coaching and Mentoring Ministries and Lady T's Design & Event Planners, LLC.

Testimonials

Are you feeling stuck? Are you unsure of your next steps in life? Do you lack confidence? If your answer is yes to anyone those questions, you should try transformation. Transformation is a process that helps you realize your potential, teaches you to appreciate your successes and grooms you into the woman you want to become. The leader- Coach Tina Frazier pushes you to dig deep during every session, which forces you to deal with your hidden issues and to discover your hidden talents. I highly recommend this process; I guarantee that you will be better after doing the work.

Thank you,

Dalicia Blount

* * *

Transformation with Coach Tina Frazier has catapulted my personal development and helped revamp the way I view myself and life entirely. If you're struggling with self-doubt, confidence, feel lost, or just have plain stinkin' thinkin', the Transformation class will give you the necessary tools to change the trajectory of your life. It is here where you will strategically learn to speak positively at all times, clearly define your desires, set specific goals for yourself and so much more. Coach Tina Frazier challenges you to dig deep and not only identify the areas of life that have formed your negative thought process but to confront them head on. I would recommend Transformation to any woman who's looking to do just that, transform!

Best,

Rachel Moore

* * *

Transformation Tuesday is what I'd like to name this journey. This time of transformation has tremendously impacted many areas of my life. Coach Tina's love, push, guidance and instruction throughout this class has shaped my self-esteem in an insurmountable way. As a result, I am very intentional in speaking only positivity over my life. I have been challenged to transform and renew my thought process and tendencies daily. Transformation Tuesday has also mobilized me to demand more out of my life. Coach Tina has helped me to produce a hunger in myself where I am no longer content with just the status quo. My perspective has changed! Transformation is not an overnight job, but an ongoing process. "Transformation is an inside job that causes for intentional watering". This is not at all an easy process; however, Coach Tina Frazier has made it a process that is worth fighting for.

Thank You,

Eboni Branch

Bibliography

Cameron, J. (1992). *The Artist's Way 25th Anniversary Edition.* New York: Tarcher Perigee.

Chernoff, M. &. (2019). *1,000 + Little Things Happy Successful People Do differently.* New York: Penguin Random House.

Courtney E. Ackerman, M. (n.d.). Retrieved from Positive Psychology: www.positivepsycholog.com/introspection-self reflection

Hammond, K. L. (02 June 2019). *Life Coach.* Delaware.

Harra, C. (n.d.). *Affirmation.* Retrieved from www.huffingtonpost.com.

Harris, R. (2011). *The Confidence Gap.* Colorado: Trumpeter Books.

Judith Belmont, M. (2019). *Embrace Your Greatness.* CA: New Harbinger Publications, Inc.

Maxwell, C. (October 6, 2014). *Shifting Negative Thoughts to Positive.*

Meberg, M. (2005). *Living A Life of Balance.* Tennessee: Thomas Nelson.

Partow, D. (2004). *Becoming The Woman I Want to Be.* Minnesota: Bethany House.

Sayers, L. E. (2017). *Mastering the Mindset of Self-Love.* Think Positive Journals.

www.ingramcontent.com/pod-product-compliance
Lightning Source LLC
Chambersburg PA
CBHW081328190426
43193CB00044B/2882